HOW TO SELL ON

AMAZON

FOR BEGINNERS: 2023

Easy Strategy Guidebook on Seller Central FBA, FBM, & KDP

ADAM WILKENS

i

TABLE OF CONTENTS

DEDICATION

This book is dedicated to my daughter Tessa Rae Wilkens

INTRODUCTION

Even with the harshness of Covid-19, which "paid the world a visit" unexpectedly in 2020, Amazon has been one of those tech giants that has stood its ground, appearing to be unmoved by the effects of the Pandemic to date. Asking why this is true defies common sense, as the restriction placed by governments of various nations on their citizens drove everyone into the online space. People who ordinarily would have preferred to put on luxury dresses to check into a shopping mall for just a body lotion had to order them online. Until the restriction was later relaxed to allow people to move about with masks on their faces, no one dared move beyond their streets (except for certain public servants and persons on essential duties).

One of the major highlights of that era was that it helped millions of jobless people across the world discover they could earn money without working under anyone. Since people were not going out to their offices or other physical places of interest, the boredom resulting from sitting idly at home forced many of them to make the internet their friend. While surfing the net regularly, many of them stumbled on tons of job opportunities online, on various platforms.

One such was Amazon. As damaging as the effects of the Pandemic were on businesses, the company offered over 100,000 people new jobs in March 2020 alone. This was according to a disclosure by Amazon in May 2020.

People found out there were a lot of things they ought to have been doing on Amazon to earn money, especially as a side hustle, while they worked their 9-5 jobs before Covid-19.

People discovered that they could create almost anything and sell them on Amazon, without leaving their homes - all done for them. This made many show interest in Amazon. While some people succeeded in making money as soon as they got started, many others struggled to make a penny or didn't at all.

So, What Was the Problem?

Trying things out yourself is good. However, when you encounter some challenges along the way, and you discover you are just not getting the desired results, you need to ask: "What are the others doing to succeed?" That can change your story.

For some people, the best way to go about this is to ask a friend or a close relative (who may know just a little about it or be entirely uninformed but pretend to be an authority). Some others would prefer to find people who have succeeded and try to copy what they do, from a distance. That also is a disaster waiting to strike.

For you who are fortunate to have a copy of this book, you'll be going through some of the proven strategies employed by successful sellers on amazon to generate a lot of money. This often happens on autopilot - they simply build a system or structure that continues to earn them monies for as long as Amazon is sustained as a marketplace for their products. A report by Amazon software provider,

Helium 10, revealed that about 50% of sellers on Amazon make around $1,000 to $2,500 monthly.

Covid-19, besides denying people their freedom, saw them lose their jobs. Businesses that primarily needed to operate physical machines to produce what they offer, folded up within months.

Amazon offers some amazing features, making it the destination of most online product sellers. Amazon's community of workers (contractors) who are committed to fast product delivery to shoppers, is one main reason why sellers are attracted to the marketplace. There is also the high royalty factor. For book publishers, for example, the royalty rate paid by Amazon is very high, especially when compared with rates offered by other marketplaces.

Let me stop the rituals. You are here to learn how to sell on Amazon. We will be looking at the very strategies successful sellers are implementing currently. No outdated tactics that do not align with current market realities. Let's get started.

CHAPTER 1: SELLER CENTRAL /FBA VS. FBM

Almost all Amazon sellers stick with one particular sales technique. On Amazon, the word "fulfillment" is used to represent the technique or approach of sellers to deploy the sale of their products.

A key differentiator among Amazon sellers is the fulfillment method they select: Fulfilment by Amazon (FBA) and Fulfilment by Merchant (FBM). Amazon stores today are mostly sellers who opted for the FBA technique.

What's the difference between Amazon FBA and FBM?

Fulfillment by Amazon (FBA) is a technique in which a seller sends their products to Amazon's warehouses. Amazon then stocks the inventory and ships it directly to the purchasers of the products, on behalf of the seller.

Fulfillment by Merchant (FBM) is a method of fulfillment on Amazon in which a supplier lists their merchandise on Amazon, and manages all logistics, including delivery and customer support.

Which Fulfillment Approach Is the Best?

Both approaches by Amazon sellers are great. A seller just needs to know what approach can suit their business goal and objectives.

For this reason, we need to talk about some things which are relevant to the subject matter.

Amazon Dropshipping

Dropshipping is an arrangement that allows sellers to promote products online, without having to buy or keep inventory. Your job is to function as an intermediary on Amazon, promoting products for other sellers and ensuring the delivery of the products to customers. From time to time, you will need to communicate with the supplier, ensuring that the orders are delivered on time and the entire process runs smoothly. Once a purchase is successful and the customer pays, you simply take your share of the money and forward the rest to the supplier.

Amazon Wholesale Business

In Amazon's wholesale model, the vendor purchases products in bulk immediately from the producer at a wholesale price after which they make a profit by selling the products on Amazon.

Amazon Private Label

Amazon personal label is about finding a product on Amazon that has a high-income potential but maybe could use some product improvement. You then find your supplier and make your product by developing your very own brand.

Let's move back a bit to what we were discussing earlier.

FBA is more suitable for brands selling on Amazon. Consumer service, high royalties, and customer support are the top motives sellers consider before choosing FBA.

As far as cost is concerned, FBA is less expensive than FBM because Amazon has first-rate freight fees inside the United States and passes them directly to the vendor/FBM seller. Amazon handles the delivery of goods and customer service for FBA sellers.

On the other hand, FBM is the best option for you in case you are selling large or heavy products like furniture because FBA isn't made for large products. Another reason to consider FBM is that you run out of FBA inventory and want to use FBM as a backup plan.

Let's discuss the advantages and disadvantages of fulfillment to help you decide which one suits your Amazon business model or operations.

Fulfillment by Amazon (FBA)

PROS:

- *Focus on Selling Alone*

Hiring, training, keeping an inventory, and shopping for subcontractors to deliver goods, and will be handled by Amazon. All you need to do is to promote the products and get customers to buy them. Nothing more.

FBA allows sellers to scale without difficulty because they do not need to worry about running out shipping goods to customers. Orders can be processed 24 hours a day because Amazon is managing all fulfillment. Because of the level of coordination, the company already has, it is better to rely on them to handle most areas of your operations. That increases your chances of being successful.

- *SEO*

Amazon helps to promote offers by FBA sellers more than FBM sellers. This is because of Prime. The level of visibility the former has on search engines is usually higher than the latter simply because customer trust is higher in products with a Prime offer.

- **Customer service**

 As we already noted, while you operate FBA, Amazon covers all of the customer service and delivery fees for any order. This reduces your overhead cost.

CONS:

- ### *Limited Control*

With FBA, you cannot walk into the warehouse to inspect your products, and it's most unlikely Amazon will let you go to their facilities for inspection. You need to trust that Amazon is delivering nothing but quality goods. However, now and then Amazon does ship out a defective unit. If you are the type that is overly concerned about quality delivery to your clients always, then don't consider FBA.

- ### *Packaging and Labeling*

Amazon has strict rules for FBA sellers on the packaging and labeling of goods before such goods are accepted into the Amazon inventory. So most FBA sellers are usually not too sure whether or not their new products would be accepted by Amazon. Whereas, with FBM, you keep stock of your goods. It doesn't matter whether they are of low or high quality. This is simply because Amazon won't know.

Fulfillment by Merchant (FBM)

PROS:

- ***Inventory Control***

FBM offers you management over your inventory and fulfillment techniques. Sellers enjoy more flexibility in inspecting their goods to confirm their quality.

For many sellers, owning the entire consumer experience process is important. Using branded packaging and self-made marketing tactics is what they prefer. All that is allowed with FBM. Inserts into applications are most effective and feasible with FBM.

- ***Fewer Charges***

If your organization is already set up for dropship and you feel you have a high level of skill and competency you may want to stick with FBM.

If your transportation cost and that of other logistics are lower than FBA's costs for the kind of product you sell, then you pay less and save costs. It is advisable to always put that into consideration when deciding on your fulfillment method on Amazon.

CONS:

- ***Buy Box Eligibility***

All different elements being the same, FBA offers will beat FBM offers for the buy box.

FBM sellers can enhance their odds of winning the buy box with the aid of offering Seller Fulfilled Prime (SFP). Just notice that FBA will nonetheless have a slight facet over SFP when it comes to the buy field, but SFP shipping costs can be a great deal higher than trendy FBM.

If buy box opposition to your products is hyper-aggressive then FBA is probably the better route.

- ***SEO***

FBA offers are given better chances to be found in search engines compared with FBM offers. No special keywords give them such a ranking in search engines. With little or no SEO efforts by FBA sellers, their offers would still find the way to the top easily because Amazon somehow helps to give them the boost - this is unannounced, but we have noticed Google Shopping tends to favor Prime offers.

- ***Customer Service and Delivery***

With FBM, the merchant handles customer support and delivery, which may come with higher costs as stated previously. Because Amazon already has a robust network of delivery guys (subcontractors) in place. Delivery delays are less likely to occur. This is why most sellers on Amazon opt for FBA (Seller Central).

What to Consider before Opting for FBA

* The products you sell are small and lightweight

* You're okay allowing the customers (shoppers) to communicate directly with Amazon's representatives on your behalf

* You would like Amazon to handle your customer support

* You are likely to run out of stock quickly and or don't want to manage your inventory

* You do not have good logistics knowledge

* Delivery cost would be more favorable if Amazon undertakes shipping to the customer instead

What to Consider before Opting for FBM

 * You want more control over your customers

* You have a great customer support service already in place

* The products you promote are large or heavy

* You already have logistics covered

* You feel you may not run out of stock too quickly

CHAPTER 2: MOVING FROM VENDOR CENTRAL TO SELLER CENTRAL/FBA

Issues with purchase orders (an official document issued by Amazon expressing their intention to pay the seller for the sale of products) are often the reason why sellers may want to cross over from Vendor Central to Seller Central.

But What Is the Difference Between the Two: Vendor Central to Seller Central?

We have discussed FBA and FBM, right? If you truly took the time to understand their difference, then you have nothing more to worry about. FBA and FBM are used to describe the fulfillment type themselves while Vendor Central to Seller Central refers to the categories into which Amazon puts them to reflect their business models. They are separate platforms.

When you opt for Vendor Central, you are called a "vendor." Amazon buys your products from you, then resells them to their customers. This also implies that you sell directly to Amazon, they own the goods.

Before we delve into the steps you can take to switch, let's briefly look at some critical things you need to understand to help you in your decision-making, just in case you want to switch.

Brand Protection

As a vendor, you are liable for protecting your brand. You don't want some sellers to list counterfeit or low-quality versions of your product on their store. The best way to prevent unauthorized promotion or usage of your products by sellers is by enrolling in the Amazon Brand Registry. A few advantages of enrolling in the Amazon Brand Registry include:

- Extra control over the information on product pages that uses your brand name.

- You will get the right to report any seller who counterfeits or uses your products without your permission.

Now let's move on to what steps you should take if you feel the Seller Central (Listing on the Marketplace) is more favorable to your operations than the Vendor Central model (being a supplier directly to Amazon).

Steps to Switch from Vendor Central to Seller Central

Step 1. Notify Your Vendor Manager

Ship all outstanding purchase orders or cancel any remaining open orders. Even if you do not tell your buyer, You will need to allow the PO system to recognize that you will be denying current and or future orders.

Step 2. Create a Seller Central Account

Registration for Seller Central is open to the general public, and creating an account is equally easy. Below are quick steps to follow to help you create a Seller Central account:

1. Visit https://sellercentral.amazon.com

2. Click on "Learn More"

3. Select "Sign Up".

4. Enter your email and click 'Create a New Account

5. Choose a business location and business type

6. Enter your details

7. Enter your billing information

8. Confirm your Identity

9. Add your existing Vendor Central ASINs to your new Seller Central store by searching for the ASIN's in the 'add item' tool. This can also be done via bulk operation using an inventory template.

Step 3. Select Your Fulfilment Technique

Now, you want to determine how you get products sent to your customers. You know why you are registering. Pick the Seller Central option (FBM or FBA), which best suits your business at present. Sometimes it's a good idea, and it's easy enough, to create an FBM offer and an FBM offer by creating separate seller SKUs for each ASIN. This way you have a backup fulfillment model and do not necessarily need to pick which path to go immediately.

Step 4: Set Your Prices

As a marketplace (Seller Central) seller, you've got complete control over the pricing of your products. It's indeed a great opportunity for your business to make more profits. That flexibility means a lot to so many sellers. With this added control, it is a good idea to study the pricing of your competitors. Be careful about what prices you come up with as too high of a retail price leads to fewer sales while bringing it too low may mean no profits in the end. You need to know your profitability.

Step 5. Manage Your Inventory

Inventory control is taken care of by using Amazon on Seller Central as stated earlier. Although you have become an FBA/FBM seller, it is advisable you still monitor your products and stock levels always.

Step 6. Manage Your Content

Vendor Central and Seller Central are not the same. For example, the A+ content you uploaded on Vendor Central will not appear in Seller Central. You have to re-upload your content. You can import your files via an API connection, to help you keep your content and pricing up-to-date.

Step 7. Taking into account Advertising/Marketing Options.

Most advertising alternatives are available to sellers on both Vendor Central and Seller Central. For a few vendors, Amazon looks after all product-associated advertising on its market. As an FBA seller, that is now for your management. Seller Central is intended to be 100% self-service.

Step 8. Keep Tab on Your Performance Progress

Selling via third-party on Amazon gives you complete control over your products, in addition to their overall performance. For that reason, Seller Central provides analytics at no cost. You can now see your page views and conversion rates amongst others. Such insights can then be used to help you optimize your product listings.

Step 9. Mark ASINS inactive in Vendor Central

Review each vendor code for offers on every ASIN in Vendor Central and change their availability to "Permanently unavailable" in the catalog menu. Create a case and let amazon PO management stop sending orders. If you continue to receive purchase orders you can opt for hard rejection on any orders for up to 4 PO cycles to stop new orders in Vendor Central. We then have to wait until Amazon has burned through all of their existing inventory before they relinquish buy box control to your new 3rd party offerings in Seller Central.

What Happens After You Switch?

- *Pricing*

You've got control over your pricing and can set the fee of your product as you wish. However, competitive pricing also calls for tracking your competitors, demand stage, and different elements, so that you can regulate whilst necessary.

Success options: you have to determine what fulfillment method you need to succeed on Amazon. FBA or FBM? It's up to you.

- ***Stock Control***

Sellers have greater control over their inventory and are accountable for preserving it. You'll calculate your stock turnover so that you can predict when you need to restock. See the inventory planning report.

- ***Customer Service***

A seller ordinarily should be busy interacting with customers. There are usually complaints from dissatisfied shoppers about products you have sold to them. Some of them may want a refund or just to enquire about the usage. Attending to these shoppers can take a lot of your time. In case you opt for FBA, Amazon will manage customer service for you.

- ***Accounting***

As a seller, your monetary obligations are extra. You have to manage income reconciliation, tax compliance, and so forth. Keeping records of your income, expenditure, and profits are going to also help you evaluate your progress in the business.

Tips for Identifying the Best Products to Sell on Amazon

Getting the right kind of product to promote on Amazon is instrumental to your success on the platform. And that's why we need to discuss this.

Finding what to promote on Amazon isn't pretty as easy as just searching for anything that comes to mind on Google and expecting to stumble on "the bomb" that will make you successful as a seller in the marketplace. No, it doesn't work that way. There are at least two to three things to put into consideration before you come up with something worth investing in.

You will be doing yourself a great privilege to pay greater attention to this section. This is because product selection is the first stage in the Amazon business model. Read on.

Follow these tips to help you find the right products to sell on Amazon:

1. Never Compete with Amazon

Amazon sells tens of millions of its products and understands how to get customers better than you. Besides that, their private label brands are so popular that Amazon at this point will still rank over you on Google or any other search engine, even if they stop applying SEO and other ranking techniques.

Competing with Amazon is just a wasteful venture. I am not saying you can't beat them at this, but why should you stress yourself when you have less difficult options to take on? If Amazon is already promoting a particular product, don't attempt to promote this same product. You risk wasting your efforts and losing your capital.

Amazon will outprice you by selling at insane rates and nearly always have the buyer's interest ahead of your brand because of the reputation they have built with customer trust. Once you notice that Amazon is already promoting a product you intend to promote, quickly move away from it. Do new research to get another less competitive product. That's your sure bet.

Recognition of extra niche gadgets as opposed to frequent products. You'll have higher success dominating a marketplace for less competitive products than going after your more competitive ones, particularly existing products promoted by Amazon. There are a ton of things to sell on Amazon, so there should be no serious challenge with coming up with something different. The golden rule: flee from getting into a "fight" with big brands.

2. Do Keyword Research

Proper keyword research can help you find the most suitable products to promote on Amazon. While looking for the right product to sell on Amazon, you are faced with the challenge of finding a product in high demand. Ideally, you need to sell products with high demand but less competition. You're going to do a whole lot of research to locate the golden possibilities. To find demand, you're going to need to have a look at particular keyword phrases with keyword research tools. Here are popular tools you may use:

Amazon Search Bar

Type a product into the Amazon Search bar and wait to notice what comes up. Amazon will suggest products based on search intent. If different people regularly look for the same thing, it'll appear higher on the list.

Jungle Scout or Helium 10

Both of these companies offer unique keyword research tools which can help offer insight into traffic trends and also areas of opportunity for underserved product searches. All information that can help with product development.

Google key-word Planner

Use Google Keyword Planner to locate what people are looking for online. With this tool, you can discover search interest, i.e what questions shoppers who want the type of product you sell are asking Google. Such information will help you create very effective content that can generate traffic to your store when you eventually publish. You can research for and make use of other keyword research tools to find what internet users are typing into the Google search box.

3. Don't Compete with Popular Brands

Amazon only isn't the big name out there you should avoid competing with. Many other brands like Gucci have become household names. They are just too popular not to get people's attention whenever they launch new items. Of course, they also follow many of the strategies we cover in this book, but it is always certain their effort will yield results, unlike a regular person. This is not to mention several other factors they can use to kick you out easily, including, lower prices, quicker delivery of goods to distant destinations, more than enough cash to spend on product promotion, well-coordinated Customer Support, and the like. Just do not consider competing with a large household brand. It's not wise at all.

When you are about to promote any product, do enough research first to be sure these kinds of brands are not standing in your way. Once you find out any of them have started promoting what you intend to sell, then drop that particular product for a less competitive one.

4. Be Sure the Product Is Profitable

A profitless venture is a wasted effort. Yes, it's okay that you do keyword research and discover the right products that give you a better chance of selling among your many competitors. It is good you follow the last piece of advice given here that you should avoid competing with the "big guys" at all costs. But of what use is all that if in the end, you are not going to make profits? This is what you should always consider when trying to find a product to sell on Amazon. It's a normal thing, right? Of course, it is. However, if you don't carefully consider your finances before choosing a product, you end up becoming a victim of a profitless venture. This is why, as a seller or a potential seller, you need to put some costs into consideration before you finally settle for a new product you will be selling on Amazon.

Consider manufacturing expenses, storage fees, packaging costs, and delivery charges. All these are very important to look at one after the other. The total, which is your cost of production, should be deducted from what you regard as your net profit. The difference (your profit) should be a major determinant before you start selling the product.

Even if you find a golden opportunity (a popular product with less competition) on Amazon, you may not make a dime if you do not sit down and do some calculations. I suggest you always use the amazon revenue calculator, which can be googled for the exact link. With this tool, you can figure out what all your seller fees would be for FBM vs FBA

5. Go for Products with Many Reviews

Opinions of customers about a product are just too useful in finding a great product to sell on Amazon. Even the more successful sellers on Amazon won't live to tell the tale if they're no longer continuously bringing in high-quality reviews.

Examine the comments of shoppers about the product before investing. Clients who love a particular product will probably make a repeat purchase. They are also going to mention the reason why they will regularly need such products. If a product is regularly needed, then it is worth considering. Additionally, if a great product has repeat bad reviews you can use that as an opportunity to improve or fix it.

The strategy is simple: look out for products that already have tons of positive reviews. Read what each shopper is saying about them, as much as you can. What you should take from them all is: will this product be demanded often? If yes, you've found it!

6. Check the Product Size

On Amazon, smaller products are more easily handled than larger ones due to storage challenges. This is particularly for vendors and sellers who deal with physical goods. Heavy items will be more expensive to store and ship. Don't forget this while you're researching new products.

Think about selling athletic shorts—those are lightweight and can be compressed into the dimensions of a tennis ball. They're reasonably priced and much easier to deliver. That ease is exactly what you should be looking for. Distance barriers can be one reason why a seller may be unable to deliver a product on time. But it is less common with portable goods. The time needed to package and transport lightweight goods is lesser than compared of heavy goods, which may stay long at shipping terminals before they are moved. Smaller items also have fewer storage, shipping, and warehousing fees which add to the seller fees. Smaller items generally have fewer seller fees as a percentage of the selling price.

7. Choose a Product that Allows You to Sell Similar Varieties

While you're choosing what to promote on Amazon, try to think about the big picture. If you find success on the platform with a product, what's going to be your 2nd or 3rd product? There is the possibility of a product selling so rapidly at the beginning of the year, then suddenly demand the same ASIN collapses towards the middle of the year - not necessarily seasonal products. Certain unprecedented things may lead to such development. That is why you should not put all your eggs in one basket. Try to spread the risk.

If you are into male wear, for example, you have a wide range of clothing materials you can sell. This is not so with products like freezers or office staplers.

The way to recognize what to sell on Amazon

It's important to note, that you'll want to do your research on transport costs and supplier costs, so you understand how much you may need to spend on your item. This info lets you narrow your selection - - for instance, a two-to-three-pound object could be lightweight and easy to ship, which could assist in decreasing your shipping charges.

Along with weight, you will need to consider merchandise that is not easily breakable while you're transporting them. This can down the road lead to high returns.

Additionally, most products on Amazon range between $10 and $50 -- so you'll need to pick items you could sell for distinctly reasonably-priced, and still, be profitable.

If you've decided you are comfortable with the transportation costs -- and that your product in all likelihood falls within a healthy range -- here are 5 ways to discern what to sell on Amazon:

1. Research Amazon.com.

Manually study popular merchandise on Amazon -- which could help you decide which product you want to sell -- you may need to begin with Amazon's best-seller list by category. Ideally, once you discover a category and sub-classes, you will narrow down on a niche.

While you check out Amazon's best sellers list, you may also study the "customers also bought" segment to get thoughts for comparable merchandise.

Once you make a list of products take a look at Google keyword planner to look whether the merchandise has ample search volume, which suggests a stage of demand. As a substitute, you can use Sellerapp's product intelligence tool in particular for Amazon. Sellerapp offers a seven-day unfastened trial, which permits you to start investigating popular products on Amazon via keywords to further slim your listing.

2. Search for Products in Your Niche

Two popular chrome extensions will help you conduct keyword research on Amazon; one is Jungle Scout, which indicates your monthly sales volumes on products, presentations products with low competition, and allows you to save products to monitor them over the years. Jungle Scout's analytics let you fast and effectively slim down on a product or an industry in which you may excel. However, Jungle Scout services can get expensive, specifically when you are just starting.

Unicorn Smasher is an AMZ Tracker free alternative -- while the information isn't always as accurate as Jungle Scout, and it lacks some of Jungle Scout's state-of-the-art features, it's a helpful free choice to accumulate predicted month-to-month sales and estimated monthly sales revenue for Amazon products.

3. Discover a Need in the market

You might come upon an opening on Amazon via easy organic search -- for instance, If I search for "ladies leggings" there are over one hundred results, but when I seek "cycling leggings girls red" there are hardly 1,000.

That is a simplified example, however once in a while, you need to slender down your product search to locate a place to make an impact on Amazon. Plenty of humans are already selling leggings, but there is probably a popular fashion, color, or form of legging this is lacking on the site.

As an alternative, you could find a gap within the market by studying client evaluations of your product marketplace area of interest. Even if there are plenty of products just like yours already, you may discover that customers are unhappy with most of the current brands and want something different.

4. Go for Less competition

If you're seeking to sell a product that currently has 100,000 search results, it is probably going to be very hard to stand out in a sea of results that look identical. Seek to discover a niche inside a bigger market that has much less opposition, which guarantees your product will be easily found in search engines.

For instance, let's assume you need to sell cookbooks. "Cookbooks", as a search term, has over 70,000 results.

Instead, the search term "Cookbooks for immediate pot cooking" has at most 3,000 outcomes. Now you have not targeted the most frequently searched term, however, it's a greater focused keyword -- if someone searches "Cookbooks" they may suggest anything from "youngsters cookbooks" to "vacations cookbook". If someone searches "Cookbooks for immediate pot cooking", however, they may be more likely to organically locate your product at top of page 1.

5. Search for Categories with at least 3 results with a Best Sellers Rank (BSR)

Amazon's Best Sellers Rank (BSR) reflects each current and historic sale of an object -- so a low BSR indicates that the product is in demand for, which is important. But, in case you discover a product in a category has excessive BSR (high number), and none of the alternative gadgets have excellent rank either, this may be a sign the item is not viable.

It is important not to just pick any product to sell. It is also important not to only focus on products that catch your interest because they may not be viable. We have encountered many brand owners who have great product knowledge but the products they are selling are non-competitors or such low relevance that customers just aren't looking for the item.

If you can find something that checks all the boxes and has a keyword ranking in at least 10 terms (directly related to the item type) within the top 100,000 keyword volume by month, it is likely a viable product.

CHAPTER 3: YOUR USPTO TRADEMARK & HOW TO ENROLL IT WITH AMAZON BRAND REGISTRY

A Trademark is a business name or logo. It is good to have a name or a hallmark with which your clients can easily identify you among your competitors. Building a great brand is also as good as your success on Amazon, as a seller. To achieve the best sales and brand protection, your brand needs to be registered with USPTO (the United States Patent Trademark Office).

The USPTO is the agency that grants U.S. patents and registers trademarks to businesses or brands. It is responsible for the protection of inventions and brands. In other words, as a brand owner, a peculiar tool to help increase sales is to register your trademark with the United States Patent Trademark Office (USPTO).

By registering your trademark, you must ensure that your trademark is not sharing a close resemblance with other registered trademarks. If you accidentally encroach on a registered trademark, you will be forced to pay a legal fine as well as pay damages to the owner of the originally registered trademark.

The process by which you register your trademark can be quite complicated. You just have to get an attorney and file a trademark application to The United States Patent Trademark Office. Although, if you are based in the United States, you do not need an attorney as the process is not complicated.

Getting your USPTO trademark allows you to enroll in the Amazon Brand Registry. The Amazon Brand Registry is a service that helps Amazon users to safeguard their intellectual properties and materials, prevent bad listings, and ensure successful business growth.

Some users sometimes do not pay attention to this service, thereby missing out on some special benefits the Amazon Brand Registry offers. Some of the benefits are stated below:

* Being a part of the Amazon Brand Registry ultimately allows you to secure your property on Amazon. With its very effective tool, it helps detect early and easily any kind of infringement on your

brand and it ensures that these trespasses are stopped before they affect your brand or even your customers.

* Brand Registry offers an advanced tool that allows users to report any suspected infringement in a few clicks. These reports are acted on speedily and the brand is protected.

* Through the Amazon Brand Registry, users get access to reach out to real people for help, advice, and assistance in tackling issues and violations, ranging from listing issues to right violation issues and so on.

* By preventing infringement and tampering, the Amazon Brand Registry makes it possible for customers to see accurate information and details about your products and brand.

* FBA sellers enrolled in the Amazing Brand Registry can also take advantage of Amazon tools to grow their brands and increase product sales.

* Enrolling in the Amazon Brand Registry comes at zero cost. Or say, the only cost is a registered or pending trademark.

* Ability to use A+ content, upload videos, enroll in Vine, and access a brand analytics dashboard.

Today, over 700,000 brands in about 20 countries of the world are registered already.

How You Can Get Your Brand on the Amazon Brand Registry

First, to be eligible to register for the Amazon Brand Registry, your brand must have its trademark in the nation you want to enroll in. Users must be able to verify and authorize ownership of the trademarks.

A pending trademark application made through the Amazon IP Accelerator is also accepted. However, the trademark should be in the form of a text-based mark, also known as the word mark, or an image-based mark, also known as the design mark. For the text-based mark, the brand name on the application must correspond with the trademark text, and in the cases of the image-based mark, the images need to be uploaded just as it is on the trademark record.

To then sign in, you need to sign in using your Seller or Vendor details. In the case of an authorized agent, trademark owners need to first sign in to the brand and then the agent can include an account as an additional user. Users must use the same username and password for the account. This enables you to access the benefits the Amazon Brand Registry offers Seller and Vendor services.

After successfully signing in, up next is brand registration/ enrollment. To enroll a brand, the brand must have a unique brand name and a trademark which should appear on all the brand products and properties.

However, in the case of a pending trademark, in enrolling the brand, you will need to provide the trademark application number which is provided by the Intellectual Property Office.

After this is done, you need to create a list of product categories in your brand's product type that it should be enlisted in.

When all these are completed, Amazon Brand Registry verifies the trademark and all the provided information and details. Once this is done, you get access to all the aforementioned benefits and features that Amazon Brand Registry offers brands.

CHAPTER 4: PHOTOGRAPHY, A+ CONTENT, VIDEO & BRAND PAGE GUIDELINES, AND RECOMMENDATIONS

A+ content refers to a digital brochure on the detail page in the form of modules that distinguish your brand from all other brands on the platform - your logo, branded pictures/images, and videos you used to stand out. Some brands are tempted to want to unduly make use of Amazon's identity, and so the company has some guidelines for every seller who wishes to be unique in the marketplace.

If you do not understand these guidelines, you may hurt your account in the process. But using your A+ content properly can help you build a strong brand over time. With it, you can tell your brand story to customers - explain who you are, using images and videos.

Let's discuss some of these rules/restrictions briefly.

Amazon A+ Guidelines

- *Pricing/Promotion*

Amazon does not permit including pricing or promotional details in your A+ content. Words like "shop with us", "add to cart", and "free" must not appear in your promotion campaigns.

- *Time-sensitive Details*

Using words like "now on sale", "latest", "new", and "buy now" can get you into trouble. Other calls to action or false claims can also get you into trouble.

- *Customer Review*

Amazon does not allow sellers to reveal reviews or testimonials by customers on their A+ content.

- *Photograph and Text Formatting*

On Amazon's requirement for A+ content, images, and pictures must comply with the below rules:

- The usage of blurry or low-quality pictures and images with watermarks or content that cannot be read on mobile phones is not allowed.

- Image File Types: jpg and png (RGB Colorspace)

- CYMK color space is not supported

- File Size: below 2 MB

- Resolution: at least 72 dpi

- Animated images like GIFs are not allowed

- *Content Restrictions*

* Logos and copyright symbols are acceptable if they're of the specified sizes by Amazon.

* Amazon does not accept any hyperlinks or language aimed at redirecting shoppers to third-party sites. They do not want any "outside linking"

* As stated earlier, Amazon doesn't allow sellers to imitate or use logos, pictures, sales copies, or any other item associated with the company.

CHAPTER 5: AMAZON ADVERTISING PPC MANAGEMENT

Amazon PPC which can also be called sponsored ads is an established marketing platform that assists sellers to intensify their product sales online. PPC simply means pay-per-click. It is an arrangement where the seller only pays Amazon when people click on the ads. There is no need for you to pay for impressions if you run PPC ads.

If you supervise and optimize your PPC campaign well, you will greatly boost your product visibility and sales. This will also increase your product's organic ranking and help ensure long-term success.

What Are the Various Types of Amazon PPC Ads?

There are just three (3) categories of Amazon PPC ads namely:

I. Sponsored Products Ads: This kind of ad appears in search results and product listing pages.

II. Sponsored Display Ads: They appear on search results, on detail pages for other ASINs, and on third-party websites and apps.

III. Sponsored Brand Ads. They are only available to sellers who have joined the Amazon Brand Registry. They carry your brand logo and other personal emblems.

Understanding PPC Software Management

You could either manage ad optimization manually on your own or you could use the software. PPC software or pay-per-click software is a tool that aids businesses to regulate, vary, and record the performance of their marketing operations. The software helps users optimize their campaigns using bidding amounts and budgets. Moreover, the software allows users to manage ads or promotions on other sites such as social media

Skills and Tools Required to Operate PPC Software(s)

The below skills are needed to operate PPC software(s):

1 Time management skill

2 Analytical skills

3 Technical skills

4 Organizational skills

High-Ranking Amazon PPC Management Software and Tools

Without details, here are a few reliable software and tools which sellers can use to maximize the opportunities presented by PPC:

- Bidx
- Perpetua
- PPC Scope
- Revenuewize
- Ad badger
- Sellozo
- Zon.Tools
- Teikametrics

How does Amazon PPC Auction Run?

The Amazon PPC auction operation is easy. A default bid is submitted by each advertiser and they compete against each other for ads spot. It might interest you to know that the bid set by the highest bidder is not necessarily the cost-per-click (CPC).

For example, let's suppose you have bid $1.50 for a particular keyword and the second-highest bidder has a default bid of $1.00. As the highest bidder, know that you will win the ads spot but you will not have to pay $1.5. You will only have to pay 0.01 more than the other bidder. This means that you will end up paying $1.01 instead of $1.5.

This implies that the cost-per-click (CPC) for a particular keyword or targeted ASIN (Amazon Standard Identification Number) depends on the highest bid but isn't at all the time the highest bid.

Are There Any Benefits Attached to the Amazon Pay-Per-Click System?

Advertising is not the initial thing that comes to mind when someone mentions Amazon. It might surprise you to know that, over the years, the retail colossus has become a giant in the advertising space, globally.

Though Amazon has not unseated Google or Facebook, it has quickly improved its market dominance over the years.

You may want to ask why there are a lot of people, especially sellers, currently making use of Amazon PPC. The answer is straightforward - the huge return on investment.

Because Amazon is a retail enterprise, people who input a search term already intend to buy a product. They are functional customers that desire to make a purchase. The ads you make are more likely to convert to sales when the client is already in the marketplace for the commodity.

Many retail shops have had to shut shop and customers turned to online retail to purchase their necessities and meet their regular needs. This is because consumer data is continually increasing. Proof of this is Amazon's annual revenue figure of $469.822B which is a 21.7% increase from 2020!

Amazon PPC has an attractive consumer base that appears to continually increase more and more every year. By the use of Amazon PPC, you are targeting that consumer base. There is money to be gotten if the PPC campaign is carried out well.

So, When Can You Start Running an Amazon PPC ad?

Another question that customers have is when to launch Amazon PPC. Unfortunately, there's no definite answer to this question. We strongly advise that you launch Amazon PPC ads immediately after you create a new listing.

You need to continue to manage your bid changes within each ad to get a positive result because the CPC bid prices are very fluid. Early on in a product life cycle it is difficult to get much awareness and this is where Amazon PPC comes in, it helps you give a solution to that problem.

How the Paid Search Works

Below is a precise summary of how Amazon's paid search works. Amazon gets millions of searches every month ranging from short-tail to long-tail keywords. These searches are only from shoppers who are willing to buy a product on Amazon.

Please, understand that not all clients are in the market to buy the item right then and there, some window shops. It is normal to get clicks without sales. However, it is important to realize the goal is to increase your organic relevance. This list of products is displayed by Amazon towards the top of the results page.

However, there are what is called 'paid search results' which are displayed above the organic results regardless of what you search. The notation of the word "sponsored" will be shown next to these item results, which is how it can be distinguished on-site. Sponsored = Ad.

Even though they are usually positioned above the organic results, they sometimes do appear in between the organic results, on the right side, or at the bottom of the organic search results.

The concept of paid search on Amazon is very simple. Amazon uses an optimized auction-based strategy where sellers set their everyday budget to buy ad space on Amazon. The higher a seller or businessman or woman is ready to pay for his or her ad the larger the chances for the ads to be displayed.

Moreover, after the ad is displayed, the vendor or seller pays an amount every time a buyer clicks the ad. That is to say, they pay for advertisement per buyer click. According to CNBC, Amazon made $31.2 billion in revenue from ads in the year 2021. This tells you the impact of such ads on more product awareness and accelerated sales!

Sponsored product ads: This class of ads is displayed in organic search results and product listing pages. Sponsored product ads are very effective for obtaining high click-through rates and consistent sales conversion.

How do You Set up a Sponsored Product Ad?

STEP I: Apply for Sponsored Product Ad on Amazon.

STEP II: Select a product.

STEP III: Choose the keyword terms which should be related to the product.

STEP IV: Choose the negative keywords where you don't want the ad to make impressions.

STEP V: Be sure to select relevant keywords to match the type.

STEP VI: Assign a budget.

After these steps, Amazon will then focus your funded ads on an appropriate audience, automatically.

CHAPTER 6: HOW TO LEVERAGE SALES, COUPONS, AND OTHER PROMOTIONS TO GENERATE SALES

Naturally, in every business line, customers would always want to buy a product when there is an incentive given. It stimulates patronage. If you want to sell more on Amazon, don't hesitate to start utilizing this strategy. Capitalize on this and see your sales grow faster than you imagined.

Buyers love discounts because humans love "free". Let me paint a simple picture here. When you walk into a store to get a single candlestick sold for $0.50, but then you find a tag on the full pack saying "Promo! Get this pack of 10 candlesticks for $3." What comes to mind immediately? Even if you never planned to purchase a full pack, you may want to consider doing that simply because you would be getting the candles for a lesser price. Many buyers, like you, who walked into that shop that day would be tempted by the offer in that tag. This is an amazing sales appetizer that sellers use to increase their sales. Learn from this. By giving little discounts on products you offer on Amazon, you will begin to get a lot more shoppers to come to your Amazon store. They don't like your face, not even your name - they are after the discount. It's a powerful lead magnet that works perfectly well.

Use promotional codes as a strategy to get shoppers on Amazon to come for your products. When shoppers see promotional codes that give, say 40% discount on a product, they feel less disturbed about the cash they are about to part with. Why? Because if they do not get such a product as soon as possible, they may never be able to get it for that rate again until a long time. Limited Time! It is a psychological / customer behavior that is easy to monetize. It's human nature to feel like you missed out, or that you must act now to get a deal price. The only time it will not work is if the customer just does not have enough money to buy the item. No loss there.

How Do You Go About the Promotion?

Be Careful with Discount Rate: Do your Math and come up with a discount rate that will not completely affect your expected profit. Most discounts are usually between 5% and 49%. Be careful not to give too much discount that you end up not making any profit from the product, even if it's peanuts!

If the actual market price of a pair of shoes is, for instance, $700, you can decide to give a 10% discount and sell it for $630. That little 10% discount can be a motivation to a potential shopper. They win, you win. You guys somewhat share the profit.

Promote Offers on Social Media: Run Facebook and Instagram ads whenever you want to give discounts. It helps you maximize the opportunity as you get to reach more people. Your spending on ads is strategic - it can help you make more than 10x the spending. If you don't have the money to run ads, go ahead and post about the offer, using quality videos, sales copies, and pictures. That will make your post very catchy and help get you, buyers, too. From inside seller central you can book a social media promo code. It's great because you can track its performance just to the audience you provided the code to.

Pay Bloggers to Promote You: Let bloggers help you make noise about your new products. You can first hire a writer to write about your product, then reach out to bloggers to get it published on their blogs. To increase your chances of getting lots of shoppers to visit your Amazon store, work with blogs that already have high traffic.

Also, ensure you promote your discounted offer only on niche blogs that post content relevant to the product you offer. If you sell laptops, but you promote your offers on a blog that writes about health and safety, do not expect any significant traffic from such a blog.

CHAPTER 7: HOW TO USE HIGH-TRAFFIC HOLIDAY EVENTS AS A WAY TO LEVERAGE NEW CUSTOMER ACQUISITION

During holidays, online consumers are usually ready to spend on presents just to enjoy themselves and put smiles on the faces of their loved ones. Jumping on this opportunity is a smart move to increase the number of customers on your list. Easter, Halloween, Christmas, and several other holidays are periods when marketplaces like Amazon buzz with so much buying and selling. You can't afford to lose out on the opportunities they present.

Initiating a self-made event for the holidays and offering incentives to encourage customers to participate is one strategy that can help you find new customers.

Sellers on Amazon can get their holiday income target and advertising techniques set beforehand. Planning ahead of holidays is one of the strongest strategies to help you increase sales and attract more customers, if well-constructed.

But What Strategies Can You Deploy to Add to Your Customer Base During the Holidays?

- **Be Specific**

Another good strategy to increase your customer base with holiday events is to be specific about which holiday you want to run a promotion for. It is possible to any type of run ads during a popular holiday and records a sudden increase in sales. The increase cannot be attributed to the expertise deployed in running such an ad alone. People naturally do a lot of buying during holidays. So, any success recorded with your promotion at such times should not come to you as a surprise.

But being specific about the holiday for which you are running your ad, say Black Friday, can double your success. This approach directs the right kind of shoppers to your cart. There is a higher chance of this category of shoppers purchasing your products when they click on your link to your store. You record lesser cases of "Abandoned Cart" with this approach as the content of your ad helps to get the attention of only shoppers who are both willing and ready to take advantage of offers available for such holidays.

Being generic with your product promotion during holidays is good, but being specific is better.

- **Learn from the Previous Year**

Develop a habit of looking back to learn from your previous promotion strategies. Try to figure out what worked and which efforts were futile or didn't yield many results. This implies that you must also keep proper records of what you do during each holiday. What promotional strategies did you deploy for which holiday? Which worked, and which didn't? How did customers respond to each strategy? Which particular customers fell for your strategies? What were the existing market realities that favored your strategies then? Do they still exist today? Will they be of help even if they do? The list can be longer depending on the objectives of individual FBA sellers. But one thing is sure: making use of the previous year's data helps you replicate success more easily than trying to be ingenious, year in and year out, risking possible failure.

Find out what you did during the last Christmas that skyrocketed your rate of turnover rate by 350%. Such a feat is possible again this year if you can look into your records.

- **Test Your Ads Ahead of Time**

Everyone knows the popular saying that he who fails to plan plans to fail. This holds for every business - Amazon FBA sellers are not exempted. To maximize future holiday opportunities, you need to map out strategies ahead of time. From your keyword research to the graphics, you are going to be using for your holiday, ensure that every item and process is checked for quality and tested to confirm they are properly set to give the desired results. It sucks when you begin to run helter-skelter in a bid to correct one mistake or the other. This late-hour approach may lead to avoidable disappointments that will cost you a lot of money and customers.

Companies, especially the larger ones, may have a big team of experts who can help contain such situations. But what about you, a single seller running your business alone? You may not be able to help salvage such a situation as the challenges may turn out to be too much and overwhelming. An Amazon FBA seller should not risk this at all. Have at your disposal all the resources needed to promote your promotion on Amazon during holidays.

The idea here is to get things started before the holiday begins. Creating awareness about your upcoming event a month or two before any given holiday isn't bad. Make sure you have a good video editor to make quality videos, a highly creative graphic designer for appealing graphics, and copywriters who can help you with catchy, SEO-based content. Getting the best hands to work with you for your holiday event helps to increase your click-through rate and then leads to more purchases from shoppers on Amazon.

- **Get New Customers from Other Platforms**

"A rolling stone gathers no moss." This line of thought is not going to help any Amazon FBA seller who is ready to gather new customers during the holidays. What helps you get new customers quickly is to become "a rolling stone." It is only when you move about from one platform to the other persuading potential shoppers to visit your store for purchase, that you enjoy speed in expanding your customer base.

Always look for new customers. Spend time exploring all possible promotion opportunities/features available within the network until you get new shoppers of your brand. As much as such advice remains valid and useful, exploring more opportunities off Amazon increases your chances of getting more new customers. Make use of your website to announce an upcoming holiday promotion for your product.

Hire professional writers from freelance platforms like Upwork, Fiverr, People Per Hour, and iWriter to help you with articles at very affordable prices. Ensure that you include the link that directs visitors to your Amazon store.

Using third-party email autoresponders, direct them first to a landing page where you collect their emails and other relevant contact and personal details. On the page, ask them to subscribe to your mailing list. The main call-to-action on your landing page should not be the "Subscribe" button - the copy on the page should first have an embedded link that sends them directly to Amazon if they do not wish to subscribe to your mailing list at the time. Restricting them from subscribing to your list can turn potential buyers off, especially those who hurriedly want to make purchases and return to whatever they were doing before stumbling on your campaign.

This is a great strategy for increasing your customer base. It gives you direct access to their mailboxes, which means you can always reach out to them to inform them about updates to the promotion or other products you offer. The bottom line is that such an approach keeps them within your reach always.

Social media also has so many inherent possibilities that, if you decide to drive traffic from it alone, you'll still get more new customers than a fellow who sits on Amazon expecting to "gather miss." Common social media platforms like Facebook and Instagram are enough to double your customer base during holidays. Hire professionals to supply you with catchy sales copies that can help convert leads to sales. Get experts to create quality videos and graphics for running ads.

Optimizing influencer marketing can equally be of great help. Simply do some research about some big names in the industry whose followers are more likely to also follow you. Reach out to them and get them to help you promote your products. Some may request money to help you do this. Regard such money as an investment that will pay off handsomely with time.

If you can afford their fees, the amount they request doesn't matter. What matters is that they can help you place your offer(s) in front of thousands (or even millions) of followers who engaged with them almost daily.

This approach, if well utilized, will help you increase sales and expand your customer base. Pages of social media influencers are always buzzing with fresh posts and interesting activities during holidays. Take advantage of this period to attract more customers.

Oh yes! Let me state this. If you do not respond to customers' inquiries on time, all of your efforts are as good as wasted. It sends a wrong signal about you to potential customers. Response time is usually very instrumental to keeping potential shoppers interested in your products. Do not take too long before you reply to a potential shopper. Remain active online during the period your promotion runs.

CHAPTER 8: MANAGING YOUR STORE WITH SUBCONTRACTORS AND VIRTUAL ASSISTANTS

When you think of how overwhelming doing every single thing discussed in this book can be, you may consider reducing the burden on you by hiring freelancers to work for you. That way, you will achieve more and equally have time for your personal life.

Many sellers often get virtual assistants and subcontractors to help them with their marketing campaigns on Amazon. It gives room for specialization, which in turn leads to greater achievements for you as a seller.

Virtual Assistant and Subcontractor: Who Are They?

An Amazon Virtual Assistant (VA) is someone who works remotely to assist you with your Amazon business. They could be employed on a full-time, part-time basis. There assist in various ways, from admin to content posting and, product sourcing, among others, based on your operations.

Roles of Amazon Virtual Assistants

- ***Product Sourcing***

They spend time on product sourcing. This is probably the most difficult of their undertakings. Leave all your outsourcing activities for the VA so that you can concentrate on monitoring results.

- ***Customer support***

Multiple challenges or complaints about your products can be addressed by your virtual assistant. Don't forget that customers get pissed off when their complaints are left unattended. I strongly recommend you delegate this task to VAs and save your brand reputation.

- ***Case Filing***

A virtual assistant assists with file management. He or she organizes all your documents so that, whenever they are needed, they can be easily found.

- ***Tracking Customer Metrics***

VAs can always track or monitor complaints by online shoppers about your products. They can help clear up less difficult complaints through FAQs and/or the Support page on your website. More difficult issues can then be directed to you.

Another thing they can do for you is to help you track your marketing campaign to see its progress. They often make use of special analytics tools to track metrics on search engines, particularly Google. Data gotten from this exercise can help you to effectively analyze the market and make well-informed decisions.

- ***Creating Graphic Designs***

For every business that understands what it takes to stand out in the market, its executives certainly do not take quality graphic designs that add color and beauty to their products for granted. Having a virtual assistant who can take up this role is a great way to increase your chances of sales on the Amazon marketplace. Don't resort to doing it yourself and making public some poor graphics.

- ***Supplying Product Pictures***

Your virtual assistant can take pictures of your products and supply attractive HD images. Such VA will serve as your photographer. You can also outsource photography to contractors on websites such as Fiverr and Upwork.

- ***Handling Shipments, Inventory, and Returns***

VAs can help gather data about your orders and provide reports about their delivery status. They also offer timely notifications to your clients confirming order submission, delivery date, and scheduling, as well as, help streamline the returns method.

- ***PPC Ads Management***

Deploying Amazon PPC (Pay-Per-Click) Ads as a marketing strategy can massively increase the visibility of your product in the marketplace. The

PPC ad is a system that allows advertisers (i.e. third-party brands) to pay for ads once they're clicked. With a virtual assistant handling that on your behalf, you could take advantage of such a marketing campaign and save your time for other productive efforts that can help improve your brand and increase sales, over time.

- ***Content Creation and Marketing***

VAs also help to write sales copies that help to gain shoppers' attention. Good sales copy, when properly promoted, can help you generate more views, thereby helping more people see your product listings, either on the Amazon marketplace or via social media. According to a popular blog, Content Marketing Institute, about 73% of major firms across the world hire somebody to be in charge of their content strategy.

Services on Amazon

Amazon subcontractors and service providers are people who also can work from home but must always be available to do any of the services and additional ones. You will find that many subcontractors have unique skill sets such as people who are catalog experts and others that just specialize in account and ASIN reinstatements. What I am getting at is do not necessarily look for one person to have all skillsets. It is not a bad idea to sub-out skills and compartmentalize. Not only to keep you out of a bad situation if the one person you count on is no longer available, but for security reasons, so they cannot cause any major interference in case the relationship sours. I always like to have different people who are good at different things; A PPC person, a catalog person, etc.

CHAPTER 9: INDEPENDENT PUBLISHING WITH KDP: INCLUDING AUTHOR CENTRAL

From the start of everything related to writing, authors have been able to self-publish books with their electronic devices – and Amazon Kindle Direct Publishing (KDP) has provided more access, making it easier and more productive for authors to get their books published without getting a middleman involved in the entire process.

It's very easy to publish your book on KDP. Many authors have found their way up there easily. It has been a very good opportunity for authors who are in search of other means of transmitting their content and have had traditional publishing roadblocks in their writing careers.

Trying to self-publish is not as easy as some people perceive it to be, though. It could be overwhelming, especially as you attempt to follow all of Amazon's publishing rules judiciously, from beginning to end, from book formatting to book launch. I will take you through the exact process for publishing books successfully using Amazon's KDP.

By the time you're done reading this chapter, you should be able to have your dream book in the Kindle Store, ready to reach millions of readers across the world. Let's start by discussing a few basic things about Amazon self-publishing.

What's Amazon KDP?

Kindle Direct Publishing (KDP) is Amazon's book publishing platform used to self-publish an online book that readers can purchase, either as an eBook or print-on-demand book. It has been marked as one of the top self-publishing companies as it superbly dominates the self-publishing book market to date. Amazon KDP has been and is still a major player in the publishing industry, currently have at least 80% of the universal eBook market.

The emergence of Amazon KDP's launch in 2007 has made things a lot easier for modern writers, in their writing careers; they are motivated to take an important decision when determining how to become an author.

Writers of all disciplines have been able to strike a balance in their careers with their writing skills. They have been able to gather more knowledge about their careers in the last decade or so with the rise in their remote writing jobs. This has brought about an explosive increase in publishing eBooks as well as print books, among others, and more through self-publishing.

What Options Are Available?

There are two options for authors in publishing their books: traditional publishing or self-publishing. When comparing traditional publishing with self-publishing options, many writers deem the royalty rates on KDP higher, and less upfront money is required to get started, but how does KDP Publishing work?

KDP Publishing is an online platform for authors to self-publish eBooks and paperback books, as mentioned earlier. For eBooks, authors can upload their book files directly and it will be immediately visible in the Kindle store as an eBook for the readers to see, purchase and download at once.

For the printed copy, authors can upload their book files; KDP Publishing uses print-on-demand technology to bring out the book in print - the paperback book. Once it's purchased, the printing costs will then be subtracted from the royalties you earn from each book sold.

Simple Guide to Self-Publishing Books on Amazon

Follow the below steps to publish your book:

1. Upload your book files to www.kdp.amazon.com

2. Publish your book on the KDP platform.

3. Readers can purchase your eBook and download it at once onto their device.

4. Readers can purchase your book in a paperback or hardcover copy as well, and Amazon's KDP platform will use print-on-demand technology to print and ship your book directly to the reader after it has been purchased.

5. Amazon will then pay you book royalties per book sold on the KDP platform.

What Benefits Come with Publishing Books on Amazon KDP?

There are many advantages attached to self-publishing your books on KDP. The Amazon KDP Publishing platform has provided many helpful solutions to the publishing industry, allowing authors to publish their books more easily and keeping them active in the sustainable book business. They now make money without having to walk down the street, knocking at every door to get their books sold.

Advantages of KDP Publishing

Worldwide Distribution

Amazon's platform is a massive opportunity for writers to reach more readers. For this reason, authors can be open to global markets across all nations of the world. No geographical restriction was placed.

Short Publishing Time

With traditional publishing, books can take a very long time before they get to the market, usually due to location or distance barriers. With Amazon's platform, the such challenge has been struck out, except for authors who are still unaware of this time-saving program. The KDP publishing model is a relief to the world of writing and publishing.

Retain Your Copyrights

Though you publish your eBook to KDP, you still have the copyrights to your eBook through Amazon's non-exceptional settlement.

Higher Royalties

With Amazon, authors can earn better royalty charges than they typically would via conventional publishing homes. Although it depends on the kind of eBook. Once the decision to sell on Amazon, royalty costs may be as high as 60%. That's way more generous when compared to other publishing platforms.

Skip Inventory

Gone are the days when authors needed to buy revealed copies of books in advance to promote them. With print-on-call technology available within the Amazon KDP network, books are printed as soon as they are demanded.

How Do You Get Your KDP Royalties?

Amazon's Kindle Direct Publishing can pay its authors through royalty expenses. There are two specific royalty fees to notice:

I. The e-book royalty prices, and

II. The paperback/hardcover royalty rates.

The royalty charge for eBooks is 35% or 70%, that is, depending on which royalty fee your eBook is eligible for. On the other hand, the royalty price for paperback books is fixed at 60% royalty price.

For each royalty fee, you'll receive the applicable % royalty fee of your book's listing price.

When Does KDP Pay Authors Royalties?

Kindle Direct Publishing usually pays your royalties to you every month, approximately 60 days after the end of the month that your royalties had been gained.

That stated, note that your royalties have to get to a specified minimum threshold before Amazon pays you. You can choose to be paid via different payment options, including direct deposit, check, or wire transfer.

KDP Select is worth mentioning here. Through the Kindle Select program, authors offer Amazon exceptional rights to promote their eBooks on the KDP platform only. That implies that the author's eBook will only be available for purchase on Amazon's Kindle platform, and the author can't use some other self-publishing platforms to distribute their eBook. As a reward mechanism, Amazon gives special incentives to the author, including useful promotional resources like Kindle Unlimited and higher royalties on books.

Exploring the Hardcover and Audiobook Options

Hardcover Books

With Amazon KDP, a hardcover book is usually printed without a dust jacket. The artwork is directly printed on the cover.

Amazon offers A fixed royalty rate of 60% is usually offered by Amazon on hardcovers sold on its marketplaces. Amazon gives you a royalty anytime a shopper buys your hardcover book through Amazon KDP and a new copy is produced to fulfill that order.

Steps to Publish Your First Hardcover Book on Amazon

Below are the simple steps to follow to get your hardcover book published on Amazon and distributed through the platform:

STEP I: Go to your Bookshelf

STEP 2: In the "Create a New Title" section, click + Hardcover

STEP 3: Enter your information for each section:

- For Details, enter your title, description, keywords, categories, and others

- For content, choose print options, upload your manuscript and cover files, preview your book, and order proof

- For rights and pricing, choose the regions/locations where you hold distribution rights and set your list price

STEP 4: After entering your information, click Publish Your Hardcover Book.

Audiobook and ACX

An Amazon audiobook serves as an alternative to the eBook and hardcover book. A seller can use the ACX (Audiobook Creation Exchange) to manufacture audiobooks on Amazon. The ACX promotes audiobooks by distributing them on big platforms like Amazon, iTunes, and Audible. It comprises special features, including the Whispersync for Voice that enables buyers to purchase your

Whispersync for Voice-ready Audible audiobook at discounted rates.

A seller can use ACX to create a digital audiobook version of their book and earn up to 40% royalty from Amazon. Visit www.acx.com for more info.

What Is Author Central?

Author Central is another tool tied to the KDP platform whereby authors can create a biography and link all of their book's titles to them as a professional authors. It adds credibility to your books and also helps readers quickly identify other titles written by the same author. You can also publish any public appearance dates and post additional information about yourself or your books here. For more information visit www.authorcentral.amazon.com

CHAPTER 10: HOW TO GENERATE MORE VERIFIED REVIEWS, MANAGE CUSTOMER SERVICE, AND REDUCE RETURNS

To understand how customer review works on Amazon, an Amazon seller needs to first understand certain helpful terms associated with a review on the platform.

It is equally important to note that not everyone can leave a customer review about any given product on Amazon. There are basic requirements to do so. One of such requirements is that a potential reviewer purchases such products. Without this, Amazon would not give room to such reviews. So, how does this work? Should you just buy anything to be qualified?

Amazon expects your spending on the marketplace to reach a particular threshold before it considers you eligible to pass a vote of confidence or a vote of no confidence on any particular product. To leave a customer review on Amazon, you must have spent about $50 on the platform in the last 12 months.

You have to meet this requirement before the platform allows you to give your opinion about any product. This is because some sellers try to manipulate the system by directing many people to the platform to give reviews about their products, even when such reviewers have never used or come across the products. This is deceptive and will not help potential buyers get honest reviews about the quality or effectiveness of the products they want to buy.

It is just normal that a person who has purchased a product before is most likely to have used it, and therefore is in the best position to either recommend it to other interested users or discourage them from buying, based on their observation. But when persons who haven't used a product begin to leave reviews about such a product, it not only creates a false impression about what exactly the product is but makes a mockery of the platform itself. I believe Amazon, considering its current status, would not want to create confusion within its network as that could discourage most of its loyal patrons from using its platform.

But I don't know if you were able to point out a loophole in this approach adopted by Amazon. The fact that I spent $50 or more on Amazon in the previous twelve months gives me the exclusive right to leave reviews about as many products as I want. Awesome!

As a result, that allows for persons who have attained the $50 threshold to leave reviews about products they never purchased or used.

Let's look at some terms used with reviews on Amazon.

Product Star Rating and How It Works?

With the following explanation, we will be looking at certain criteria used often by Amazon to determine star ratings for any given product in the marketplace.

When you come across many star ratings for different products and services on some platforms, what you see is a reflection or an average of how many customers gave the reviews. For instance, for Product A, 20 customers give their reviews while for Product B, 100 customers give their reviews. When the platform presents its ratings for both products, you will find out that if Product A is rated 1 Star, Product B would be rated 5 Stars. Rating is based on the number of reviews for each product.

That kind of average does not apply to products on Amazon as the company uses other metrics to come up with the ratings. What are the common metrics applicable on Amazon?

First, Amazon tries to confirm if the reviewers purchased the product for which they give the review before it considers them as being honest. Again it puts into consideration the proximity of time. The closer the time the review was given to the period of rating, the higher its chances of influencing the rating. If Mr. A gave a review two years ago on a body lotion he purchased while Mr. B gave his just last week on the same body lotion. Amazon takes Mr. B's review to be more correct for the period than that of Mr. A since it is more recent and has a higher chance of reflecting current market realities.

Also, the platform has a technical team that examines every review given about a product critically, to ascertain the genuineness before consideration.

The above are some of the basis for either increasing or decreasing the rating of any given product on the Amazon marketplace.

Verified Purchases

One of the ways by which Amazon distinguishes what it regards as an honest review from the rest is by placing the tag "Amazon Verified Purchase" on them. When you see this the next time you visit Amazon, it implies that the review has been read and evaluated by the company and can be trusted. That however does not suggest that other reviews found on the marketplace are invalid or dishonest. It just means that the team at Amazon is yet to ascertain their genuineness.

Also, notice that in our previous discussion, I stated that a reviewer does not necessarily have to buy a particular product to leave a review on it. Based on Amazon's requirements, they are only expected to have expended a minimum of $50 on the platform in the last 12 months.

Now, it is very possible that the $50 expended by a particular reviewer could have gone for other products different from the very one for which they gave a review. And this means the review might just not be honest. It's risky to count on such a review when considering the product as you can't be too sure the reviewer purchased the given product, let alone used it. This is why Amazon takes its time to check each review on the platform before considering it "verified". The content of the review itself can give enough clues as to the fact that the reviewer did use the product or not. This requires an expert to ascertain more correctly, though.

Amazon would not consider some reviews by customers to be honest simply because some customers might have purchased the products at prices different from those stated on the platform. Or because the reviewer didn't buy the products in the first place. The team at Amazon critically analyzes reviews before they label them as "Amazon Verified Purchase" or not.

Amazon Seller Feedback

On freelance platforms like Upwork and Fiverr, most sellers do lobby for feedback immediately after a transaction is completed. It's as if the pay for the product sold or service offered is not enough. They seem to be unfulfilled after every transaction until they have gotten feedback from the customer. That has become a culture on those platforms. Customers who love your work or how you treated them while they transacted with you often leave positive feedback about you.

Those who feel unsatisfied either by the quality of work delivered or your attitude towards them are most likely to keep quiet or leave negative feedback about you, which hurt your rating on the platform and consequently scare potential customers away. No seller wants this. That is why they strive hard to satisfy every customer they come by.

That's how seller feedback works on Amazon too. A seller can ask for positive feedback about them (not the product in this case) after every sale. This boosts their rating on Amazon as sellers.

However, no one is allowed to leave feedback for sellers they have never purchased from. Feedback is very important in helping Amazon determine the quality of service delivery by each seller, as well as, used to improve their seller ratings. The rule is simple: purchase a product from a seller, then leave them thumbs up or down. So, no one comes in from anywhere to "support" a friend or relative by leaving "free feedback" without ever purchasing a product from a particular seller. Period.

Strategies Used by Amazon FBA Sellers to Get Reviews

Let me talk about a few ways by which sellers on Amazon marketplace engage shoppers to get reviews for their products without violating Amazon's terms and conditions for generating product reviews. They also include techniques used by these sellers off Amazon.

1. The "Request a Review" Button

The Amazon "Request a Review" button is an easy way to get reviews from shoppers on the platform. It's a feature provided by Amazon to help FBA sellers make requests for reviews with little or no effort. You improve your chances of getting customers' reviews by simply utilizing this button. It's a way to get customers to add extra value to your profile. It is visible from inside each order ID.

Reviews are one large factor that potential shoppers consider before buying from you. And so, making good use of this feature is a step in the right direction. The button usually remains useful or accessible by any buyer who purchases your product within a 4-30 days period.

This means that, if a customer is too busy with some other personal things or initially reluctant to leave a review, you still have the opportunity to keep in contact with them about the products they had purchased from you. Amazon does, however, do this for you automatically in most cases. If you are yet to take advantage of the "Request a Review" button, now may be the best time to consider it.

3. Take Part in the Amazon Vine Program

The Amazon Vine Program is one sure way by which a seller can increase the chances of getting more reviewers on the platform. It is a faster way.

New FBA sellers may not be able to take advantage of this feature. The program is not available to all sellers on Amazon due to certain requirements associated with it. To take part in this program, a seller is required to have few to no reviews from buyers on an ASIN. Also, the seller's product(s) must have been duly enrolled in Amazon Brand Registry. Not all new sellers have a trademark, but with commitment, consistency, and the right sales/marketing strategies, any new FBA seller can find their way to the top and attain even more than 30 reviews in a couple of months. But how does the Amazon Vine Program work?

Unlike several other marketplaces where reviewers get incentives from buyers to leave a positive review, the Amazon Vine model guarantees that nothing but honest reviews are left by reviews about products. How does this work?

Amazon requires that any seller who wants to be a part of the Vine program first submit up to 30 of their products. These submitted products are then distributed by Amazon to "Vine Reviewers" for free, to test or use them and subsequently leave reviews based on their experiences with the products. This approach ensures that every review is eventually given results from actual experiences or usage by individual reviews, and not mere lip service paid to the products. This category of reviews (reviews gotten through the Amazon Vine Program) gets the tag "Vine Customer Review of Free Product." The Amazon team supervises this process to ensure it is transparent and can be trusted by customers across the platform.

Before this time, many sellers on Amazon were gravitating towards paying reviewers to review their products, allowing for dishonest reviews or reviews not resulting from true experiences with the products. Such reviews are usually misleading -

primarily the reason why Amazon finally put an end to this practice in 2016 by introducing the Amazon Vine Program with strict conditions to ensure transparency and trust in its review system. Any Amazon FBA seller that attempts to incentivize buyers to get reviews does it at their own risk.

4. Use third-party automated email responders

Although there are strict restrictions placed by Amazon on sellers regarding messages that can be sent through third-party email autoresponders, it remains a powerful tool that can help sellers gather a lot of reviews from their customers. You, however, need to carefully go through the conditions under which you can send messages to customers through a third party.

Let's look at some of the forms of messages sellers must avoid at all costs, based on Amazon's restrictions, if they wish to opt for a third-party email autoresponder:

- Do not send messages to customers asking them to adjust the reviews they had given to favor you, asking for their removal

- Friendly messages as simple as "Thank you for the patronage" can get your account flagged red by Amazon. So be careful not to send an appreciation message to your customers via third-party autoresponders.

- After you have made an initial request to a customer for a review on a particular product through the Amazon "Request a Review" bottom, do attempt to message them to review a product or remind them about initiating the review via third-party autoresponder

- Don't try to mail a customer asking them to leave a review once they are satisfied with the product purchased

- Sending messages to customers informing them about freebies or coupons will endanger your Amazon account. Promotional messages via a third party are not allowed

- Never send a message that confirms the delivery of products to a customer unless the customer asks first

- Messages that try to encourage customers to leave reviews through incentives will attract penalties. We have noted earlier that Amazon frowns at it. So, do not attempt to do this either on the marketplace itself or through a third-party email autoresponder

5. Build an Email List

Having your email list is another great strategy that can help you gather a lot more reviews without having to break the rules set by Amazon. We have already pointed out that strict restrictions are being placed by Amazon on sellers who intend to message shoppers requesting reviews via third-party email autoresponders. What then do you do in this situation?

If you have tried many other strategies as discussed in this book but still desire more reviews, reaching out to customers outside of Amazon is a great option you should consider. You don't have to meet these customers on Amazon in the first place. What is required is to promote your product through other platforms like Instagram, Twitter, and Facebook and get potential customers to go over to your store on

Amazon and leave positive reviews about you and the products they purchase. This can be achieved by adding a link that leads them to your Amazon store in a post on the said platforms. (Google 2-Step URL)

Whether it is a free or sponsored (paid) post, ensure you request that they leave a positive review after a successful purchase. You can make this more effective by running Facebook or Instagram ads with landing pages that describe the product, highlight its benefits and previous reviews left by customers, and a kind request for review. You'll be surprised by the tons of reviews you'll get using this method, especially if you set your ads to run for a longer period. Ensure you add a promotion code or other forms or incentives to achieve a quicker and better result.

With this, you get potential shoppers to purchase the products on Amazon and leave positive reviews, without violating the set rules. Let me give you an example of what a typical sales copy that would work for this strategy would look like:

"SAMPLE SALES COPY..."

Note that you need to be creative to attract the attention of potential shoppers with this method. Again, it will cost you some extra bucks - you just have to spend to get the desired result. As the saying goes, "Nothing good comes easy." This shouldn't scare you as you are sure to get your RoI (Return on Investment) within a short peperiodThe strategy gives a lot of reviews. Positive reviews mean more sales and more money for you.

7. Excellent Customer Relations

When you treat customers well, you get more customers - existing customers come back for more transactions while newer ones say "hi" when they come across positive reviews and feedback about you and the products you offer. This is always the situation with businesses that have good customer relations globally, so, cannot be debated. Treating your customers without regard, even when your products are "super excellent", will earn you a bad reputation and see your loyal clients desert you one after the other. Let's not even mention potential customers because the chances of getting any are low with poor customer relations. So what point am I trying to make?

The business of getting positive reviews and only positive reviews is a great strategy to reel in more. Nothing kills a business faster than a negative remark from a client. Avoid negative reviews at all costs. Don't even allow one - not even in this age and time. The whole world now lives on the internet. Information now travels a longer distance and seems to reach everyone in a twinkle of an eye. There's hardly any business today that is not represented online. Even startups without a product or service yet have a website.

With this consciousness, you should understand that bad reviews (which are usually left online these days) can easily result in the sudden collapse of your business. This is because they are not hidden from the public, unlike when they are given physically (verbally) or forwarded to your customer service unit in written form.

In every successful company you can find today, there exists an active and well-coordinated customer service unit. Without this unit, lots of customer complaints will be left unattended to, and that portends great danger to continue of the business. That is because customers will never be happy when you don't address the complaints lodged with your organization. Or how would you feel if you purchase a product but later discover that it's either not working or damaged already, you inform the seller but get insulted for complaining.

Dissatisfied and disappointed right? You may never want to deal with such a seller or business outfit again. By extension, you would, out of anger, want to leave a negative comment or review about them and the particular product.

When many customers visit your store, the first thing they want to see is what others are saying about you as a seller and the products you offer. Positive reviews send a powerful signal that you can be trusted or at least that you have a reliable track record that can serve as the basis for transacting with you. An Amazon FBA seller who needs more positive reviews must ensure they never have a record of a negative review.

CONCLUSION

To promote your products on Amazon successfully, you must be able to provide unique, budget-pleasant products with less competition to be able to rank on search engines. It is now not smart to sell on Amazon for the sake of promoting on Amazon alone. Rather, you want to make certain you're virtually able to generate traffic to your store from every possible platform.

If you have a product in mind to sell on Amazon, do your best to follow the strategies we discussed in this book, relevant to your sales model.

If you do not have a product in mind currently, you can find a viable one by doing some research online about products that are selling fast. Study what others are selling to create a list from which you can choose and start your business on Amazon.

Once you have got a list based totally on keyword studies, consider comparing products so you can finally settle for ones that shoppers on Amazon purchase more often.

Let me drop this final tip, which I believe is the general outlook of all that I have said. To succeed as a seller on Amazon, FBA, or FBM, explore all platforms possible. Never stay on Amazon alone to promote your products. Always look for opportunities to expand your footprint. Good luck and Thank You for reading!

EXTRA TIPS & RESOURCES

1) Free Keyword Tools: help find keywords to implement on the front and back end

• Google Keyword Planner Tool

• https://keywordtool.io/Amazon

• https://www.merchantwords.com/

• https://moz.com/free-seo-tools

• When on Amazon, search #keyword to come up with a list of other most popular keywords. For example, search #robots, then write down all of the other terms and use them on your hidden keywords or in content.

• KW Index Checker - it's an APP for Chrome. (fee may be applicable)

2) Discover what product categories or products are hot:

• https://www.helium10.com

• https://amzscout.net/

3) Track Pricing and Rank History of any ASIN on Amazon.com

• www.camelcamelcamel.com • www.keepa.com

4) Fake Review Analyzer

• https://www.fakespot.com/ • https://reviewmeta.com/

5) Generate More Reviews on Seller Central

• https://www.junglescout.com w

6) Help Removing Sellers and Navigating Brand Issues on Amazon.com

• https://potoosolutions.com/

7) Seller Forums

• https://sellercentral.Amazon.com/forums/

8) Amazon Advertising YouTube Channel:

• Visit YouTube and search "Amazon Advertising Channel."

9) LinkedIn Groups:

•	Amazon Vendor Central (AVC)

•	Amazon Seller Central (ASC)

•	Search more Amazon groups for Valuable Q&A

•	Add me on LinkedIn
http://www.linkedin.com/in/awilkens

Contact me for Consulting or Rep Services:

•	http://www.dotcomreps.com

•	Email: adam@dotcomreps.com

I would love to hear from you!

GLOSSARY

1P – 1st Party, referring to Vendor Central. Also referred to as a "Retail" vendor.

3P – 3rd Party, referring to Seller Central. Also referred to as a "Marketplace" supplier.

A+ – Also called Enhanced Brand Content. Offers a digital brochure for your product(s) on the detail page below the standard product description.

a9 – the SEO language specific to the Amazon.com platform. See www.a9.com

ACOS – Advertising Cost of Sale.

ACPC – Average Cost per Click.

Amazoninians – Describes people who work for Amazon.com. The company culture.

AMG – Amazon Media Group, the display advertising team.

AMS – Amazon Marketing Services, now called Amazon Advertising.

ARA – Amazon Retail Analytics.

ASIN – Amazon Standard Identification Number. The Amazon Standard Identification Number is a 10-character alphanumeric unique identifier assigned by Amazon.com and its partners for product identification within the Amazon organization

ASN – Advance Shipment Notification.

ASP – Average Selling Price.

B2C – Business to Consumer.

BD – Best Deal.

BIN Check – If ever you need to request an Amazon review, the correct product is in the network at the FC you would request a Bin Check. This is when their warehouse associates confirm the product in the Bin is the correct product the customer receives when they place an order for a given ASIN. It is a quality control check at the FC of inventory correctness.

BOL – Bill of Lading.

Brand Registry – Service that offers additional brand tools and protection for manufacturers with intellectual property.

Browse Nodes – The specific selling category assigned to your product. i.e., Sporting Goods→ Bicycles → Mountain Bicycles.

Buy Box – The owner of the primary sales offer on the Detail Page.

CARP – Carrier Appointment Request Portal.

CM – Category Manager, aka Vendor Manager.

COGS – Cost of Goods Sold.

COOP – Cooperative Marketing Allowance or Funding for Deals, Promotions, or Discounts.

CPC – Cost Per Click.

CPM – Technically this means "Cost per Mile," but it is most frequently used to refer to Cost Per Thousand, as it concerns advertising impressions. i.e., Cost per thousand impressions.

CRAP – Can't Realize Any Profit. A Term used when your ASIN economics have been deemed unprofitable by Amazon.

CSLD – Category-Specific Lighting Deal.

CTA – Call to Action. Marketing Terminology to prompt customers to "act" on a deal or special price.

CTR – Click through Rate. % of people whom an ad made an impression on and clicked on the ad. DA – Damage Allowance. This is an allowance in Vendor Central.

Detail Page – The independent page that houses all of your ASIN content, outfacing the customer. DMM – Divisional Merchandising Manager. Above the VM and the VMM.

DOTD – Deal of the Day. Duplicate – A double or copy of the same product with a different ASIN on Amazon.com.

EBC – Enhanced Brand Content, also called A+ content. Offers a digital brochure for your product(s) on the detail page below the standard product description.

FA – Freight Allowance.

FBA – Fulfilled By Amazon (Seller Central). Amazon ships the order to the customer.

FBM – Fulfilled By Merchant (Seller Central, B2C). Seller Dropships to the customer.

FC – Fulfilment Center.

Gateway Page – Referring to the home page that you land on for www.Amazon.com

Gating – Blocking specific sellers from reselling your products or brands.

GBLD – Gold Box Lighting Deal.

GL – The primary selling category where your products can be found on Amazon.com.

Halo Effect – The Residual Euphoric Sales Lift an ASIN has after a faster turn rate caused by a lower price or increased traffic to the detail page.

Hero ASIN – In a promotion, this refers to the ASIN's primary outfacing product exposed to the customer of a grouping. It is usually your best seller in a group.

HSA – Headline Search Ads. These ads appear under the search bar. Now called sponsored brand ads.

Hybrid – A manufacturer who simultaneously operates Vendor Central and Seller Central accounts.

IPI – Inventory Performance Index

ISM – In-Stock Manager. This position within merchandising helps with ops-related issues such as purchase order troubleshooting and forecasting.

LBB – Lost Buy Box. Amazon refers to this figure as a % of the time that you do not own the Buy Box.

MAP – Minimum Advertised Pricing.

MDF – Market Development Funding (Coop). This is an allowance in Vendor Central.

Merge – Combining two ASINs into one. Or the movement of any information from one place to another.

MSRP – Manufacturer Suggested Retail Price.

NIS – New Item Setup. Refers to the XML setup files by category in vendor central by which you can create new ASINs

OOS – Out Of Stock.

OPS – Amazon uses this term internally regarding "Sales."

PCOGS – Net Sales. This stands for the product cost of goods sold.

PDA - Product Display Ads. These ads appear on detail pages under buying options.

Platform – Also see uI. It is the name given to the Amazon.com site and sister sites.

POC – Point of Contact, refers to your main contact in an organization.

POD – Proof of Delivery (request). R

A – Return Allowance. This is an allowance in Vendor Central.

RANK – Refers to your sales rank number in a category relative to all others in that category.

RMA – Return Merchandise Authorization

ROAS – Return on Ad Spend (similar to ROI).

RR – Routing Request. Relating to shipment requests in Vendor Central.

SBV – Sponsored Brand Video Ad, formally VIS.

SC – Seller Central.

SDP – Shortage Dispute Process. Another form of POD in Vendor Central.

SERP – Search Engine Page Results.

Shoveler – Widgets on Amazon.com facing the customer that provide purchasing suggestions based on customer metrics, current promos, or best performers in a group.

SOP – Standard Operating Procedures.

SPA – Sponsored Product Ads. These Ads appear in Search Results.

SP – Selling Price.

SKU – Stock Keeping unit. You manufacturer-assigned a model number.

Store Page – AKA brand page. This is the storefront page you create for your brand (must be resisted).

Twister – Also known as a "Variation." This is a grouping of ASINs that are combined into one detail page and are differentiated by size, color, or style.

UI – user Interface. The term Amazon uses to describe any of its various websites.

Vine – Paid program for generating approved reviews through Vendor Central.

VIS – Video in Search. Amazon's latest AMS tool adds a short video as a sponsored product ad. Now referred to as a sponsored brand video

VLT – Vendor Lead Times.

VM – Vendor Manager, synonymous with Category Manager.

VMM – Vendor Manager, Manager. A manager of Vendor Managers.

VPC – Vendor-Powered Coupons

VC – Vendor Central.

VSS – Vendor Self Service, references the Vendor Central uI platform.

WOC – Weeks of Cover. Refers to how many weeks of inventory usage are based on sales.

WOW – Week on Week. Referencing sales comparing the current week to the week prior.

YOY – Year on Year. Comparing sales from one year to the next.

NOTES

_____

_____

_____

_____

_____

_____

_____

_____

_____

_____

_____

_____

_____

_____

_____

_____

_____

Made in the USA
Las Vegas, NV
25 January 2024

84869770R00075